Patches
AND STRIPES
A "VANDERBILT MAGIC" STORY

ELLEN MASON *and* ED CLAMPITT   *illustrated by* OLGA LEVITSKIY

We dedicate this book to the Vanderbilt Museum staff, trustees and volunteers, past and present, who have given so much of themselves in keeping William K. Vanderbilt II's vision alive.

-EM and -EC

To Blaze, Thank you for your constant love and support.

-OL

Text copyright © 2020 by Ellen Mason and Ed Clampitt
Illustrations copyright © 2020 by Olga Levitskiy

Cover design by Olga Levitskiy

All Rights Reserved. This book, or parts thereof, may not be reproduced in any form without permission in writing from the publisher. Library of Congress Cataloging-in-Publication Data
Patches and Stripes A "Vanderbilt Magic" Story
Printed in the United States by BOOKMASTERS, INC.,
Baker & Taylor Publisher Services | 30 Amberwood Parkway | Ashland, OH 44805
JOB # O-0001652
August 2020

ISBN 978-0-9749378-3-0

Welcome to Eagle's Nest,
The Vanderbilt home.
We are quite sure
You'll have fun as you roam.

They say there is *magic*
Inside of these gates,
So jump on our tram,
Our story awaits!

Another day starts
At the Vanderbilt gate,
As people drive through
To enjoy this estate.

Keith, Manny and Steven,
With Ed standing there,
Smile and greet them
With *kindness* to spare.

A car then approaches,
A mom, dad and son,
So happy to be here
And join in the fun!

The boy wears a hat,
An unusual type,
With bright colored patches
And blue and white *stripes.*

Like a little conductor
On a make-believe train,
He wears his hat proudly
In sunshine and rain.

"Hello, little man,
What a wonderful hat,"
Greets Ed at the gatehouse.
"Meet Max, our pet cat."

"Please park your car now
And then join me, Ma'am.
Let's all take a ride
In our brand new tram."

"It's just like a train
But without a track.
It takes guests to the mansion
And then brings them back."

"I am the tram's conductor,
Though I don't have a hat.
The one on your son's head
Will help take care of that."

Off they all go,
Glad to *explore*,
Reptiles and birds
And fishes galore.

Ed returns to the gatehouse,
Parks the tram in the back,
When Manny inquires
About their usual snack.

"Ed, where are the *donuts*
That you normally buy?
They sweeten our workday
And make the hours just fly."

"We always count on you
For a donut or two.
It's so disappointing
If you don't come through!"

"Each Sunday you bring them,
Cream-filled and *jellies*,
Which makes you our hero
In our hearts and our bellies!"

"I'm so sorry fellas,"
Ed then replies.
"It was too late this morning
To get our supplies."

A few hours later,
When he's on his rounds,
Ed meets the family
While circling the grounds.

Mom is blinking back tears,
Her voice filled with dread.
Ed sees the young boy:
No hat on his head.

"The hat has just vanished.
We watch it with *care*,
But now we have lost it
And have no idea where."

"This hat means so much,
A gift from the past,
Handed down from Great Grandad,
To our son , meant to last."

"As a railroad conductor,
He wore his hat every day
On the train that he rode on,
`Very proudly', he'd say."

"It's a family *treasure*
That we hold very dear,
Passed down to our son
From my father this year."

Ed assures the young parents,
Like a comforting touch,
"The staff here will find it.
Don't worry so much."

"We take *pride* in our work
And we make quite a crew.
Never lose hope.
We'll get that hat back to
you!"

So the staff begins searching,
From the left to the right,
As the bright autumn day
Inches toward night.

They search the grounds outside,
By the tall silent eagles,
That stand at the entrance,
Looking ever so *regal*.

They search near six columns
One thousand years old,
Brought here from Carthage
For us to *behold*.

They search by the whale shark
While it hangs from above,
As if it is swimming
In the ocean it loved.

They search among fishes
And reptiles and birds,
When all of a sudden,
A loud *shout* is heard.

"I found it!" Ed yells,
As he runs with the hat.
"I found it just now,
In the Habitat!"

"Among all the animals
That fill up the spaces,
I noticed the hat
Between the glass cases."

The family is phoned
With the news of the find.
Mom screams, full of joy,
"You have all been so kind!"

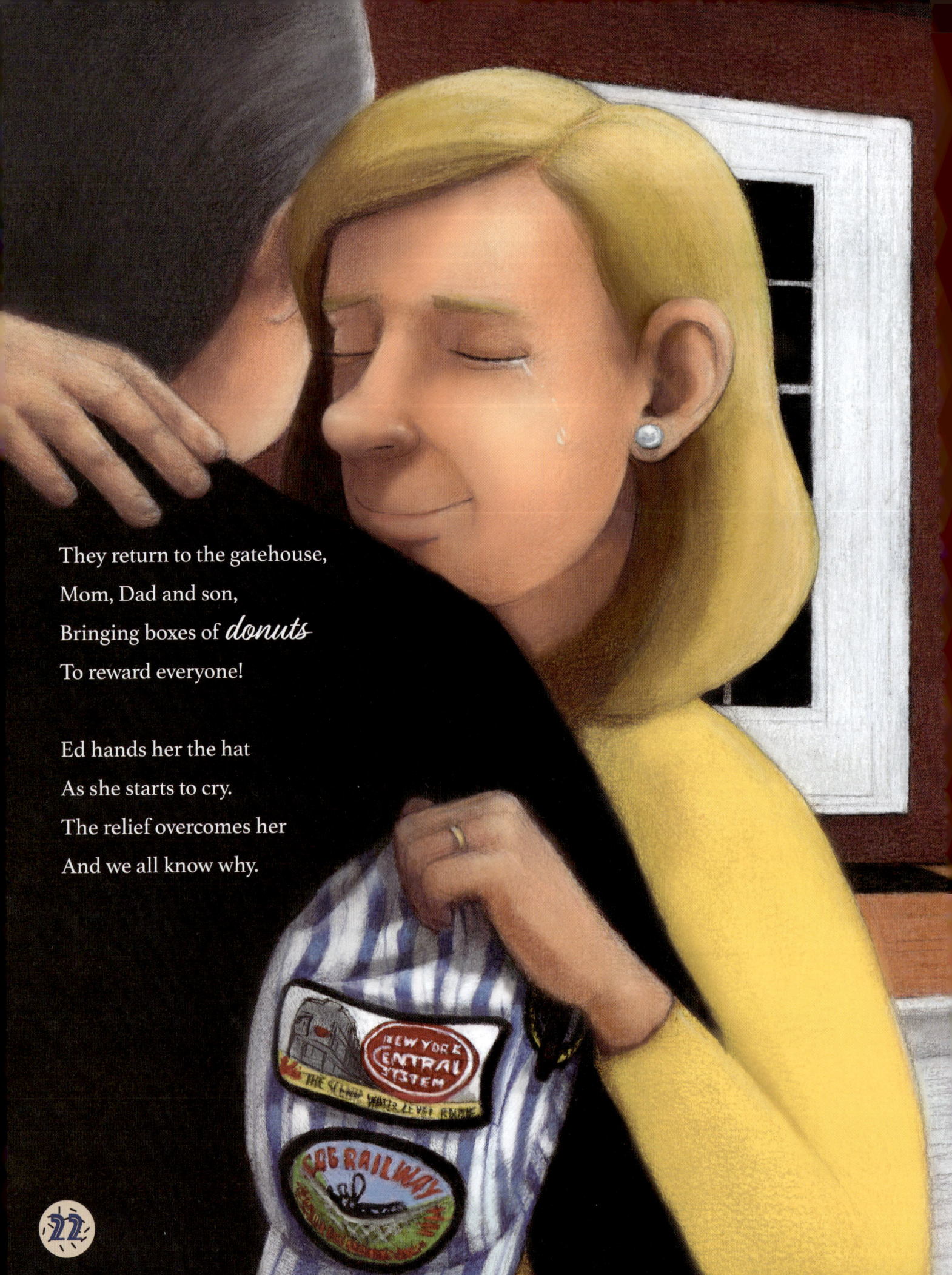

They return to the gatehouse,
Mom, Dad and son,
Bringing boxes of *donuts*
To reward everyone!

Ed hands her the hat
As she starts to cry.
The relief overcomes her
And we all know why.

She sobs on Ed's shoulder.
Tears flow like a stream.
She hands him two boxes
For the Vanderbilt team.

"We thank you with donuts,
A gift for each guard,
To show we are *grateful*.
You've all searched so hard."

"You've brought us together
With this special hat.
It's back with its owners.
What is better than that?"

Ed hands out the donuts.
Their faces all glow,
As he thinks to himself,
"How on earth did she know?"

The end quickly comes
To a *wonderful* day.
The staff waves goodbye
As they drive away.

They have seen Eagle's Nest,
This lovely estate,
Filled with such treasures,
Both tiny and great.

The Vanderbilt magic
Has touched them for sure,
With history and wonder
Behind every door.

And all these years later,
With this simple story,
We are all reminded
Of the Vanderbilt *glory*.

Of the railroad and trains,
Of Grand Central Station,
And the proud *family*
Who helped build this nation!